Made in United States
Orlando, FL
05 May 2022

17509082R10078